Rhythmic Training

by Robert Starer

STUDENT'S WORK BOOK

ISBN 978-0-88188-458-6

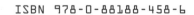

HAL•LEONARD® CORPORATION

7777 W. BLUEMOUND RD. P.O. BOX 13819 MILWAUKEE, WI 53213

Visit Hal Leonard Online at **www.halleonard.com**

INTRODUCTION

While <u>Rhythmic Training</u> supplies musical examples for the student to perform, there are two essential ways in which the book's impact can be strengthened: invention of rhythmic patterns by the student and his notation of them from hearing.

This workbook furnishes directions and space in these two areas. The student is asked to invent examples within precisely given limitations, and space is provided for dictation on the same page. In class, examples invented by the students may be used for dictation or the instructor can provide his own.

The workbook concentrates on the first six chapters of <u>Rhythmic Training</u> where the need for these additional procedures is the greatest. For chapters seven through twelve, only selected examples are given. The chapter numbers and the numbers of the exercises in the workbook correspond exactly to those of <u>Rhythmic Training</u> and the two books should be used together.

Robert Starer

PRELIMINARY EXERCISES

Invent an example using the following rhythmic values: ♩ , ♪ , ♪. , 𝅝

Write them between the upper two lines, exactly above the beat on which they occur.

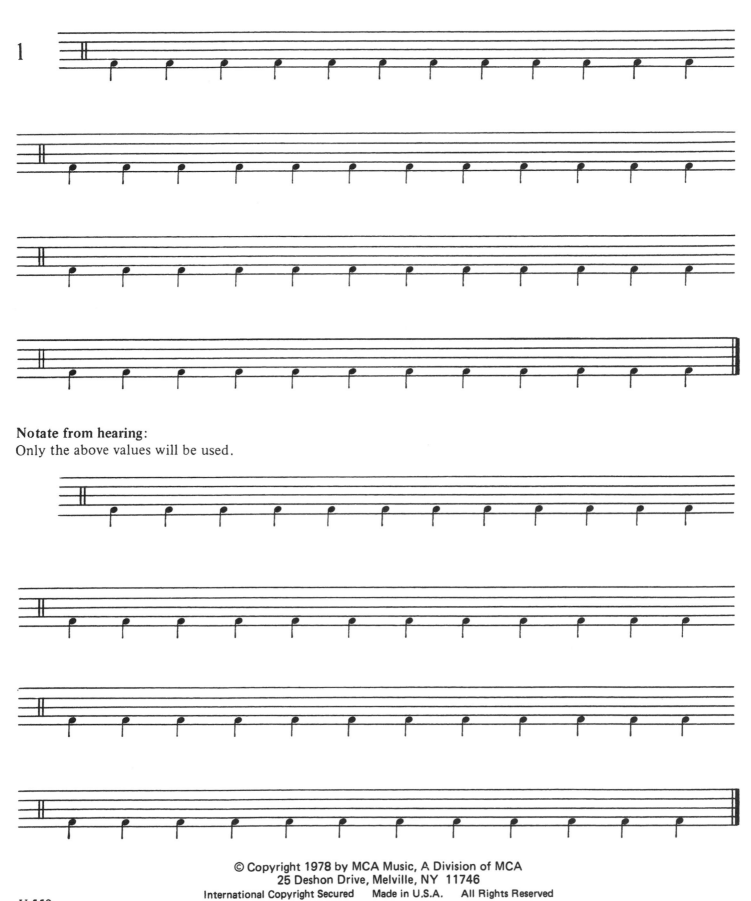

Notate from hearing:
Only the above values will be used.

Invent an example using the following rhythmic values: o♩ , o· , o·· , o͡o as well as the ones in No. 1. Use each one of the new ones at least once.

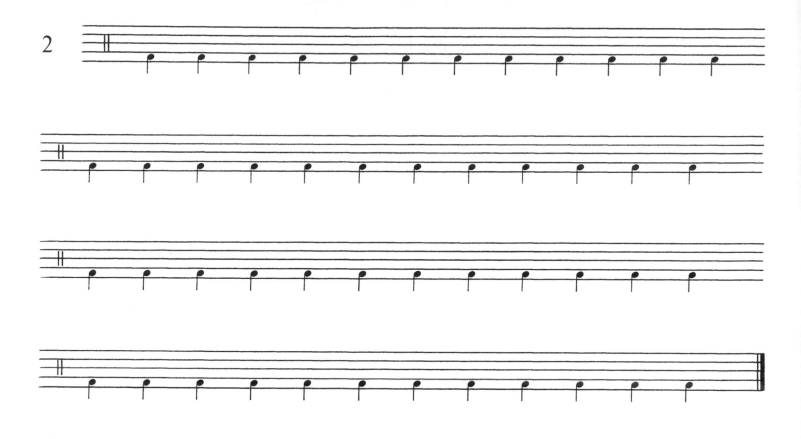

Notate from hearing:
Only the above values and the ones from No. 1 will be used.

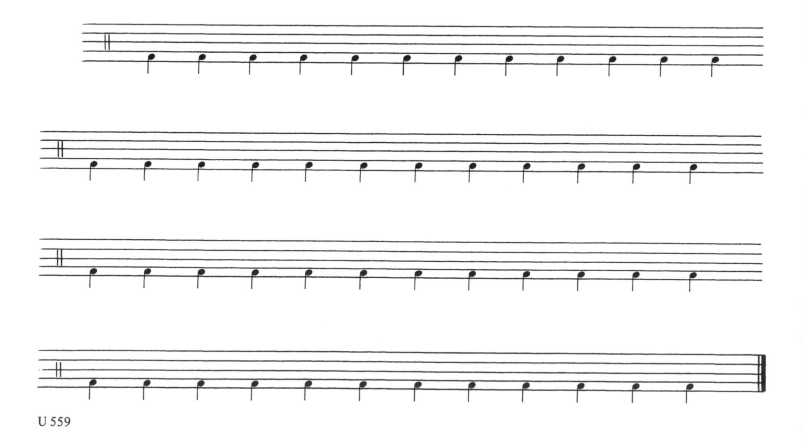

Invent an example using the following rests:

 as well as notes.

Use each rest symbol at least once.

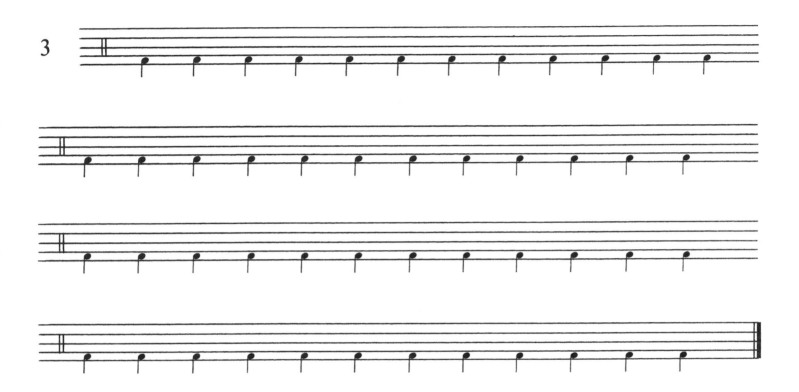

Notate from hearing:
Be sure to distinguish between rests and long notes.

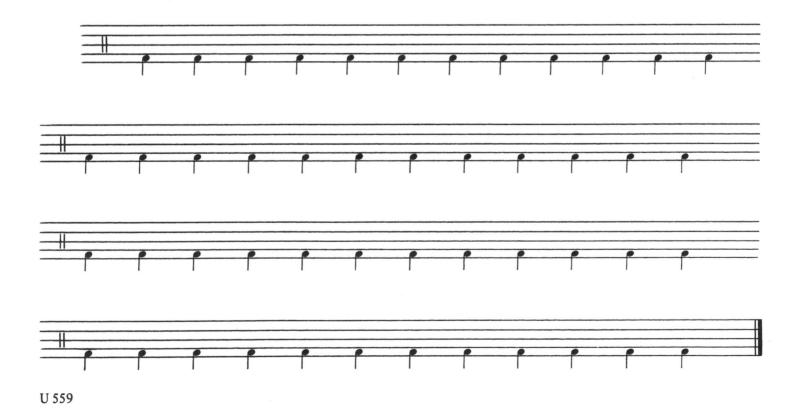

Chapter I

Invent an example in $\frac{2}{4}$ meter with the following rhythmic values: ♩ , ♩ , ♩⌢♩ , ♩⌢♩ , ♩⌢♩ , ♩⌢♩ as well as quarter and half-note rests: Try to use most of the above symbols.

4

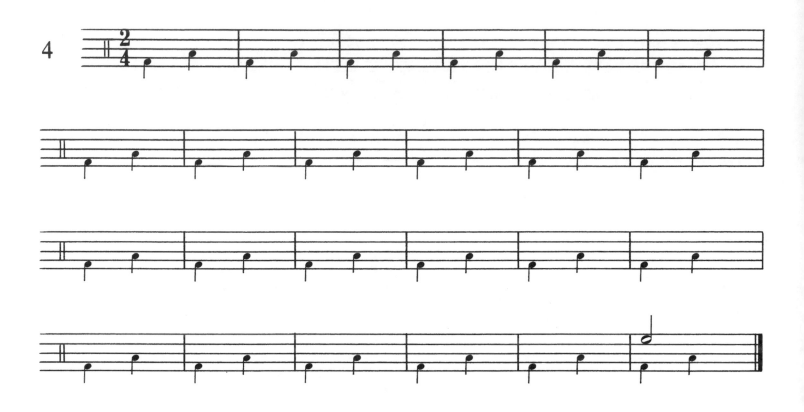

Notate from hearing:
Maintain the distinction between downbeat and upbeat.

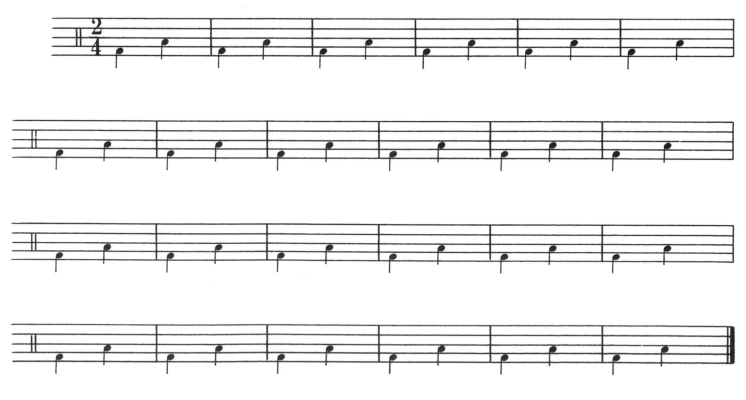

Invent an example in $\frac{3}{4}$ meter using: 𝅘𝅥, 𝅗𝅥, 𝅗𝅥.

Also use slurs that go over the bar-line from any one of these three values to any other and, of course, rests.

Notate from hearing:

U 559

8

Invent an example in 4/4 meter using ♩ , ♪ ,♩. , ○ , slurs across the bar-line and rests:

Notate from hearing:

Invent an example in $\frac{5}{4}$ meter which is a combination of 3+2:

Invent an example in $\frac{5}{4}$ meter which is a combination of 2+3:

Invent an example in $\frac{5}{4}$ meter which mixes 3+2 with 2+3: Put down the pulse and dotted bar-lines first, then make up the rhythms.

9

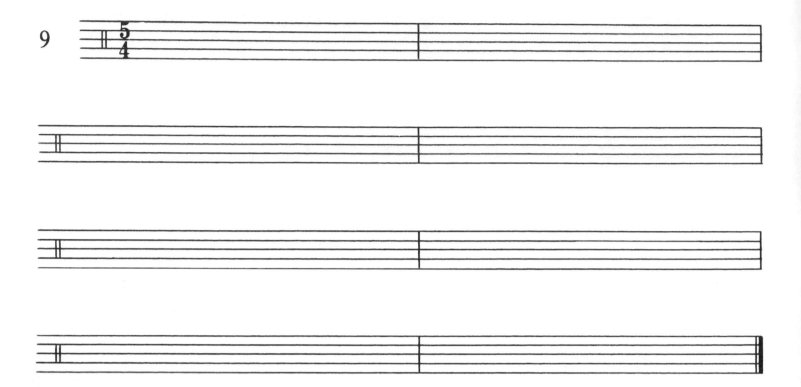

Notate from hearing:
This will be in $\frac{5}{4}$ meter, mixing 3+2 and 2+3. At first hearing notate the pulse, on later hearings write down the rhythmic values.

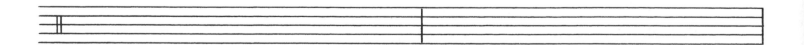

Invent an example in $\frac{6}{4}$ meter which is mostly 3+3 but has an occasional 2+2+2:

Notate from hearing:
This will be in $\frac{6}{4}$ meter, mostly 3+3, but perhaps 2+2+2. At the first hearing jot down the pulse, on later hearings the rhythmic values.

12

Invent an example in 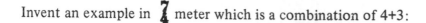 meter which is a combination of 4+3:

Invent an example in 7/4 meter which is a combination of 3+4:

U 559

Invent an example in **7** meter which is a combination of 2+3+2:

Invent an example in **7** meter which mixes 4+3 with 3+4 and 2+3+2: Write the pulse and dotted bar-lines first, then make up the rhythms.

Invent an example in which the meter changes frequently: Use $\frac{2}{4}$, $\frac{3}{4}$ and $\frac{4}{4}$ and, if you like $\frac{5}{4}$, $\frac{6}{4}$ and $\frac{7}{4}$. Give the meter indications, bar lines and pulse first, then the rhythmic values.

15

Notate from hearing:
At first, the meter indications, bar lines and pulse, then the rhythmic values.

Chapter II

Invent an example in 2/4 meter using eighth-notes ♪♪ or ♪♪♪♪ as well as quarter and half-notes:

16

Notate from hearing:

16

Invent an example in $\frac{2}{4}$ meter using eighth-notes and eighth-rests: Use each of the following possibilities at least once:

17

Notate from hearing:

Invent an example in 2/4 meter which uses syncopation: Use each of the following at least once:

Notate from hearing:

18

Invent an example in 2/4 meter that uses the dotted quarter-note.

For instance:

Notate from hearing:

Invent an example in $\frac{2}{4}$ meter using eighth-notes and rests, syncopation and dotted quarter-notes freely: Begin it with an upbeat and fill in the pulse for the last bar.

Notate from hearing:
It will begin with an upbeat and you must fill in the pulse for the last bar.

Invent an example in ¾ meter using different combinations of eighth-notes, quarter-notes, half-notes and dotted half-notes: Begin with an upbeat and fill in the pulse for the last bar.

Notate from hearing:
It will begin with an upbeat and the pulse for the last bar has to be supplied by you.

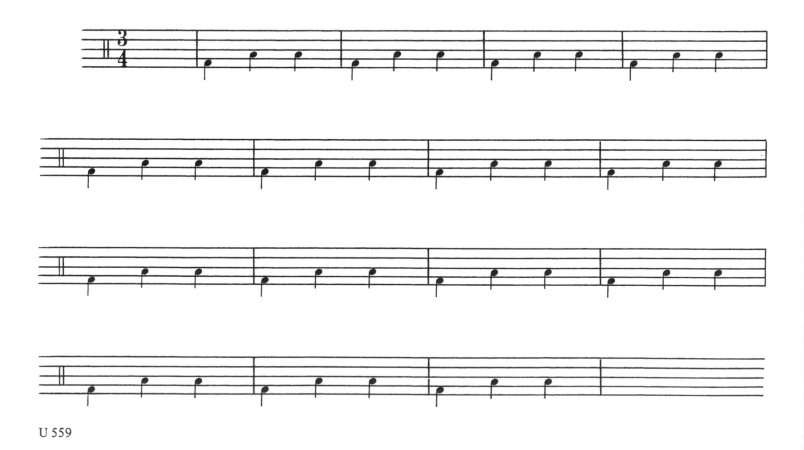

Invent an example in **4/4** meter using different combinations of eighth-notes, quarter-notes, half and whole notes and, of course, rests:

22

Notate from hearing:

22

Invent an example in $\frac{5}{4}$ meter (3+2 or 2+3) using eighths as well as other notes:

Invent a similar example in $\frac{6}{4}$ meter (mostly 3+3 but an occasional 2+2+2):

Invent a similar example in $\frac{7}{4}$ meter (4+3 or 3+4 or 2+3+2):

Invent an example with eighth-notes and frequent meter changes. Use $\frac{2}{4}$, $\frac{3}{4}$, $\frac{4}{4}$ and $\frac{5}{4}$. First write the meter indications, bar-lines and pulse, then the rhythmic values you want.

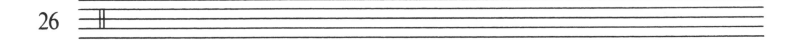

Chapter III

Invent an example in $\frac{2}{4}$ meter using triplets:
Use each of the following at least once:

Notate from hearing:

Invent an example in 6/8 meter: Remember that each beat is now ♩. Use each of the following at least once: You may also use slurs within the bar and across the bar-line.

Notate from hearing:

Invent an example in $\frac{3}{4}$ meter using triplets: Begin with an upbeat and fill in the pulse for the last bar.

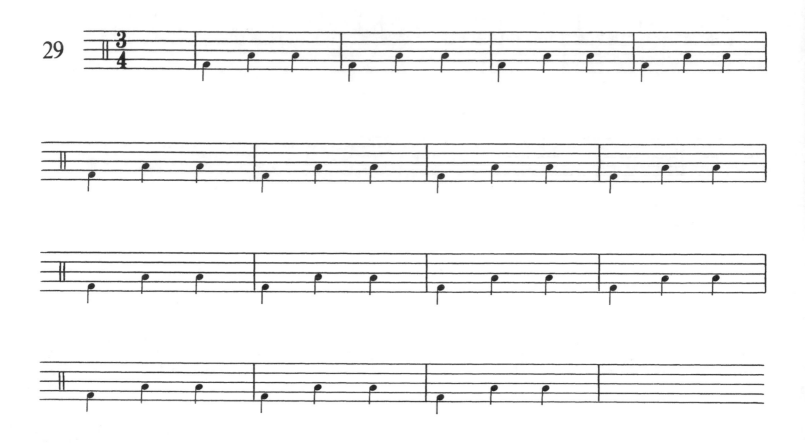

Notate from hearing:
It will begin with an upbeat.

Invent an example in 9/8 meter: Begin with an upbeat of one or more notes and fill in the pulse for the last bar.

Notate from hearing:
It will begin with an upbeat.

Invent an example in 4/4 meter: Use triplets frequently and also use half-notes, dotted half-notes, slurs and rests.

Notate from hearing:

Invent an example in $\frac{12}{8}$ meter: Use dotted half-notes, a variety of rests, slurs within the bar and across the bar-line.

Notate from hearing:

Invent an example in $\frac{5}{4}$ meter (3+2 or 2+3) using triplets as well as half-notes, dotted half-notes, rests and slurs:

33

Notate from hearing:
The combinations of 3+2 or 2+3 are the same as above.

Invent an example in $\frac{15}{8}$ meter ($\frac{6}{8}$ + $\frac{9}{8}$ or $\frac{9}{8}$ + $\frac{6}{8}$): Use dotted notes and rests.

Notate from hearing:
The combinations of $\frac{6}{8}$ + $\frac{9}{8}$ or $\frac{9}{8}$ + $\frac{6}{8}$ are the same as above.

32

Invent an example with triplets and frequent meter changes: Use $\frac{2}{4}$, $\frac{3}{4}$, $\frac{4}{4}$, and $\frac{5}{4}$.

35

Invent an example with frequent meter changes using $\frac{6}{8}$, $\frac{9}{8}$, $\frac{12}{8}$ and $\frac{15}{8}$.

36

Chapter IV

Invent an example in 2/4 meter using sixteenth-notes: Use the following three patterns:

Notate from hearing:

Invent an example in **2/4** meter using sixteenth-notes: Use the following three patterns:

38

Notate from hearing:

Invent an example in  meter using sixteenth rests. Use each of the following at least once:

Also use the double-dotted quarter-note:

39

Notate from hearing:

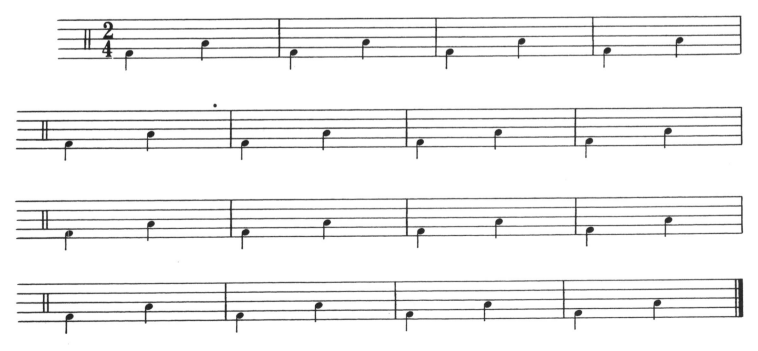

Invent another example in  meter using eighth and sixteenth rests: Concentrate on the following:

Begin with an upbeat of one or more sixteenth-notes and adjust the final bar accordingly:

40

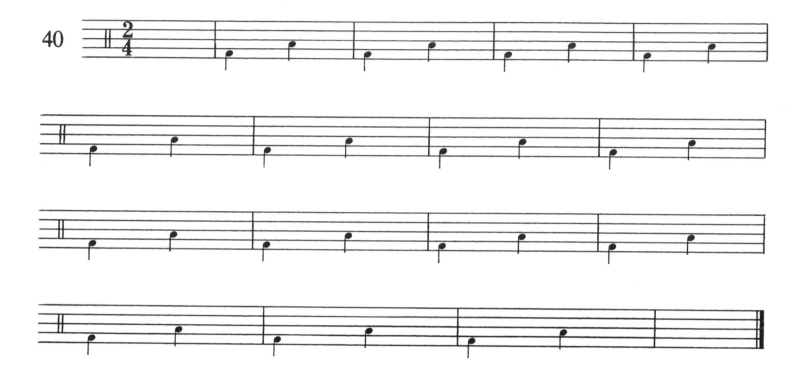

Notate from hearing:
This will begin with an upbeat of one or more sixteenth-notes.

Invent an example in $\frac{2}{4}$ meter using any of the patterns acquired in Nos. 37, 38, 39 and 40:

Also use slurs within the bar or across the bar-line. Begin with an upbeat and adjust the final bar accordingly.

Notate from hearing:

This will begin with an upbeat.

Invent an example in $\frac{3}{4}$ meter using sixteenth notes and rests. Look over the patterns given in Nos. 37, 38, 39 and 40 and try using all of them once in this and the next example.

Notate from hearing:

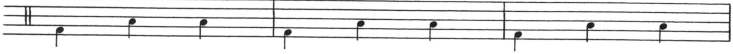

Invent an example in 4/4 meter using sixteenth-notes and rests: Begin with an upbeat and adjust the final bar accordingly.

Notate from hearing:
This will begin with an upbeat.

Invent an example in $\frac{5}{4}$ meter (3+2 or 2+3) using sixteenth-notes and rests as well as half-notes and dotted half-notes:

Notate from hearing:
The combinations of 3+2 or 2+3 correspond to the above.

Invent an example with sixteenth-notes and rests with frequently changing meter: Use $\frac{2}{4}$, $\frac{3}{4}$ and $\frac{4}{4}$.

45

Notate from hearing:
Write the meter changes and pulse at first hearing, the rhythmic values later.

Chapter V

Invent an example in $\frac{2}{4}$ meter mixing eighth-notes with triplets and sixteenth-notes: Subdivide the pulse if necessary to

by adding eighths or sixteenths to the printed quarter-notes.

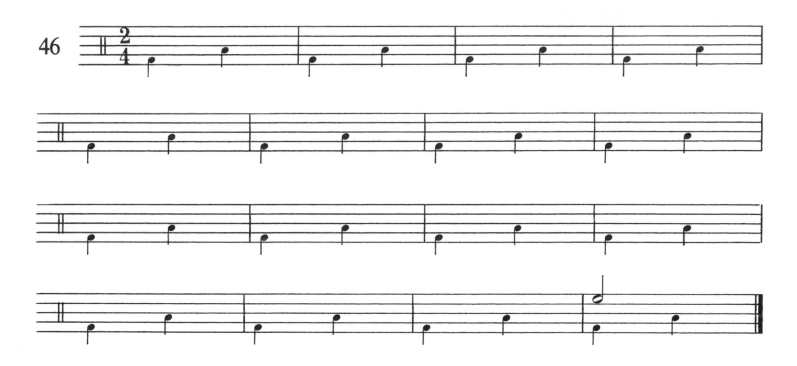

Notate from hearing:
Subdivide the beat if necessary.

Invent an example in **6 8** meter mixing different divisions of the beat. Use the following notation:

Notate from hearing:
Use the above notation.

Invent an example in 3/4 meter mixing eighth-notes with triplets and sixteenth-notes: Be sure to use rests and subdivide the pulse when necessary.

Notate from hearing:
Subdivide the beat if necessary.

Invent an example in $\frac{9}{8}$ meter mixing different divisions of the beat. Use the following notation:

Notate from hearing:
Use the above notation.

Invent an example in $\frac{4}{4}$ meter mixing eighth-notes with triplets and sixteenth-notes: If necessary, subdivide the pulse.

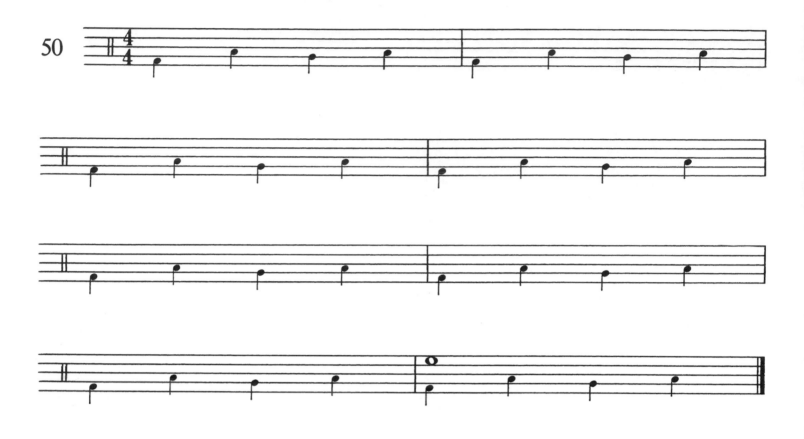

Notate from hearing:
Subdivide the beat if necessary.

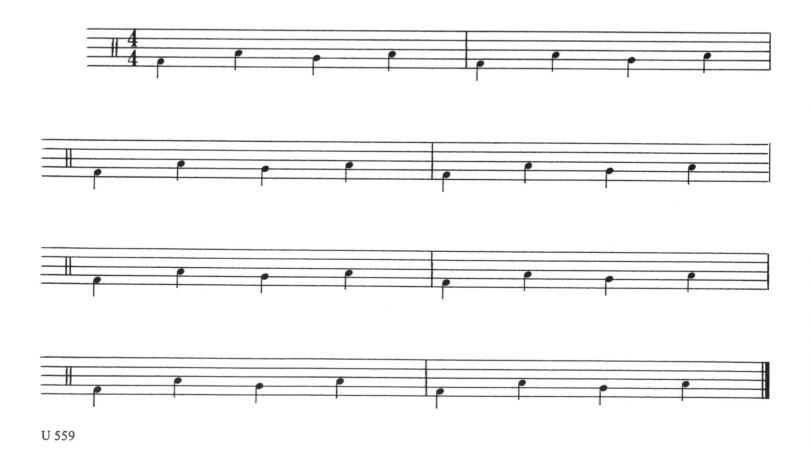

Invent an example in $\frac{12}{8}$ meter mixing different divisions of the beat: Use the following notation:

Notate from hearing:
Use the above notation.

Chapter VI

Invent an example in **6/8** meter with sixteenth-notes: Use the following four patterns:

Notate from hearing:

Invent an example in $\frac{6}{8}$ meter with sixteenth-notes: Use the following four patterns:

Notate from hearing:

50

Invent an example that uses eighth and sixteenth rests extensively as well as ties within the bar and across the bar-line: Begin with an upbeat of one or more sixteenth-notes and fill in the pulse for the last bar.

54

Notate from hearing:
This will begin with an upbeat.

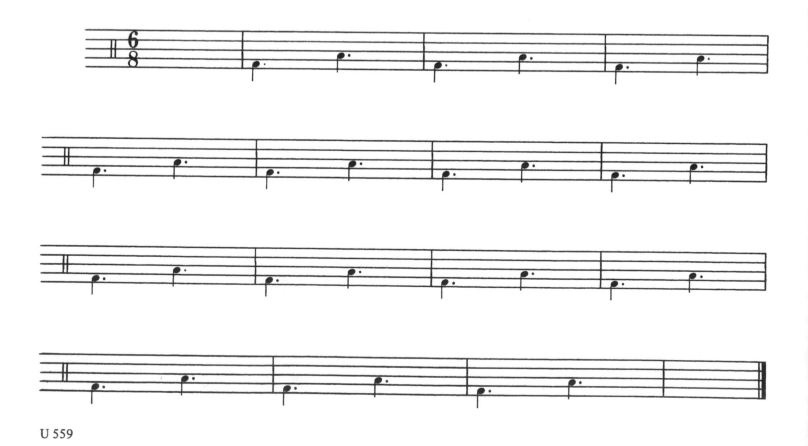

Invent an example that uses more intricate, syncopated patterns which may necessitate a temporary subdivision of the beat. Use each of the following at least once:

Notate from hearing:
Subdivide the pulse if necessary.

Invent an example in **6/8** meter using any of the patterns acquired in Nos. 52, 53, 54 and 55: Subdivide the beat when the intricacy of the pattern makes it seem advisable.

Notate from hearing:

Invent an example in 9/8 meter using sixteenth-notes and rests: Look over the patterns given in Nos. 52, 53 and 55 and try using every one of them in this and the next example.

Notate from hearing:

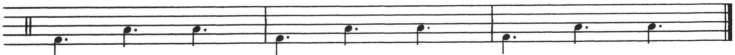

Invent an example in $\frac{12}{8}$ meter using sixteenth-notes and rests: Subdivide the pulse when you use the more intricate patterns.

Notate from hearing:

Invent an example with sixteenth-notes and rests and frequently changing meter: Use $\frac{6}{8}$, $\frac{9}{8}$, $\frac{12}{8}$ and $\frac{15}{8}$ ($\frac{6}{8}$ + $\frac{9}{8}$ or $\frac{9}{8}$ + $\frac{6}{8}$).

59

Notate from hearing:
Write the meter changes and the pulse at first hearing, the rhythmic values later.

Chapter VII

Write an example in **2/4** time with quintuplets:

Write an example in $\frac{2}{4}$ meter that mixes triplets, quintuplets and septuplets with eighth and sixteenth-notes:

Notate from hearing:

Chapter VIII

Write an example in **2/2** meter dividing the beat into eight equal parts: Subdivide the pulse as necessary.

Write an example in **2/2** meter dividing the beat into twelve equal parts: Subdivide the pulse as necessary.

Chapter IX

Invent an example in $\frac{3}{8}$ meter that uses thirty-second notes and rests:

Invent an example in $\frac{2}{4}$ meter that uses thirty-second and sixty-fourth notes: Subdivide the beat when necessary.

Chapter X

Invent an example in which the pulse changes from ♩ to ♪ and back: Write the pulse line first (as in No. 79), then the rhythmic values.

81

Invent an example in which the pulse changes from ♩ to ♪ and back: Write the pulse line first (as in No. 80), then the rhythmic values.

82

Chapter XI

Write an example in any meter you wish and use any rhythmic figuration you like, from the simplest to the most complex: Write it on the middle line and omit the pulse altogether.

86

Notate from hearing:

Chapter XII

Write a rhythmic canon in **2/4** meter in which the second voice enters one beat after the first:

94
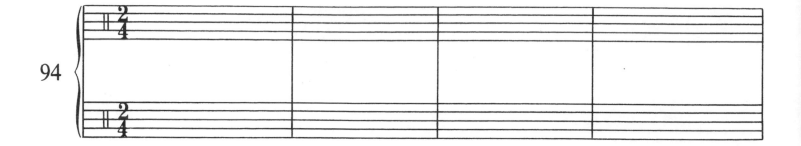

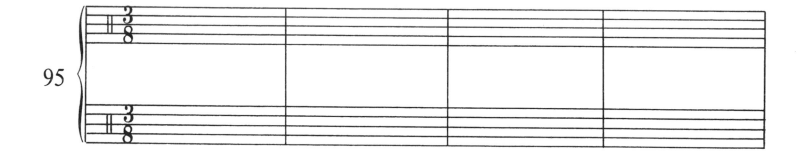

Write a rhythmic canon in **3/8** meter in which the second voice enters one bar after the first:

95
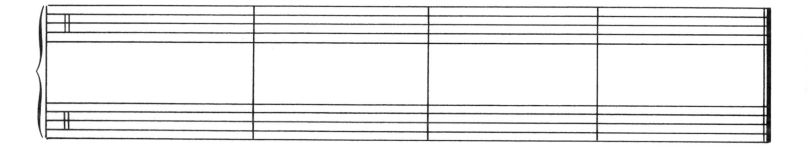

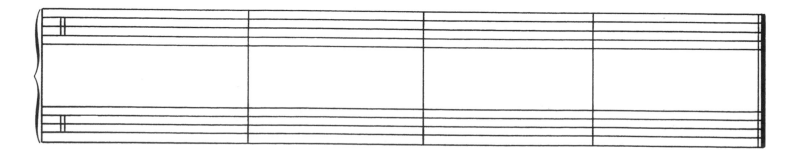